The Brave Ninja: Nasir Finds Confidence

By: Jaelyn Eley, Lynnecia Eley, and Calvin Eley, Jr.

Book Title: The Brave Ninja: Nasir Finds Confidence
Authors: Jaelyn N. Eley, Lynnecia S. Eley, and Calvin Eley, Jr.
Illustrator: Dacil Curbelos
ISBN: 979-8-3304-7618-3
First Edition: November 2024

For permission requests, email: author.jaenasir@gmail.com

To all the brave young readers,

This book is dedicated to you—

May you live with **Integrity**, Lead with **Confidence**,

Embrace your **Leadership**,

And always stay in **Control** of your own story.

You have the power to be amazing, just like Nasir!

Meet Nasir!

Nasir (pronounced "NAH-seer") loved everything about ninjas. He admired their flexibility, and most of all, their bravery.

One afternoon, while watching ninja moves online, he saw a contest ad announcing an event: the "Ninja Video Storytelling Challenge."

INJA
I AM A NINJA
NI

The challenge invited kids to create and share their own ninja stories on video. Nasir's mind raced with excitement, but a wave of nerves hit him. "What if I get nervous and forget what to say on camera?" he wondered.

Despite his doubts, Nasir decided that he wanted to participate. He spent the next few days crafting a story about a ninja who saved his village using courage and cleverness.

His dad, Ceej (pronounced "Siege"), helped him practice, saying, "Your story is amazing, Nasir. You'll do great!"

The night before the event, as Nasir practiced in front of the camera, he felt his confidence shift. "What if nobody likes my story?" he thought.

Seeing his worry, Ceej sat down with him and said, "Nasir, speaking up is about sharing your ideas and having the courage to express yourself. Remember, even the bravest ninjas feel nervous sometimes."

Ceej added, "Confidence doesn't mean you're never afraid. It means you try anyway. Trust in your story, and know that I'm proud of you no matter what."

On the day of the challenge, Nasir set up his camera, ready to record. He watched other kids' videos online, each one different and special in its own way. When it was his turn, his heart pounded.

He took a deep breath and remembered his dad's words. "I can do this," Nasir told himself, pressing the record button. As he started his story, the words just came out.

With each sentence, his confidence grew, and he found himself having fun and enjoying the experience.

REC

After he finished, Nasir uploaded his video to the online platform.

The comments from all of the viewers were positive and encouraging, and he felt a rush of pride, not just for sharing his story but for finding the courage to speak up.

Ceej hugged him tightly afterward. "You did it, Nasir! You were so brave!"

Nasir smiled. "I was nervous, but I remembered that being brave is about trying. I'm glad I spoke up, dad."

HD

From that day on, Nasir knew that bravery wasn't just about muscles and quick moves. It was also about having the confidence to express himself, just like a true ninja.

MAT

About the Authors:

Jaelyn N. Eley, at the time of this publication, is an energetic and imaginative eight year-old who is in the second grade. He loves reading books, building with Lego mini-figures, and pretending to be a ninja. His favorite superhero is Spider-Man, and he believes that with a little confidence, anyone can be brave like his heroes. Jaelyn's daily affirmations—Integrity, Being a Leader, Confidence, and Control—help him tackle new challenges every day, thanks to the support of his parents.

Lynnecia S. Eley is a best-selling and award-winning author, Confidence Coach, and proud mom. She is passionate about inspiring confidence. With each story she tells, Lynnecia strives to remind others that courage and confidence come from within.

Calvin "CJ" Eley, Jr. is a military veteran, entrepreneur, and proud dad. Since Jaelyn was 4 years old, CJ has taught him the "4 Keys to Success" as daily affirmations: Integrity, Being a Leader, Confidence, and Control. He believes that these principles will help Jaelyn—and other young readers—unlock their full potential.

www.ingramcontent.com/pod-product-compliance
Lightning Source LLC
Chambersburg PA
CBHW040102160726
48196CB00072BA/1476